G

G

g

g

Initial G

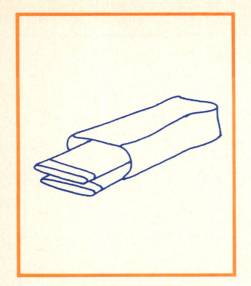

Gg

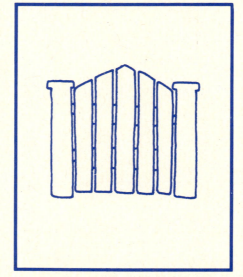

Initial G

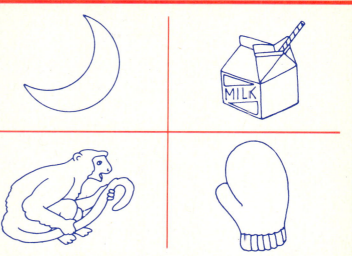

Initial M
3

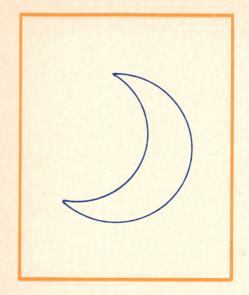

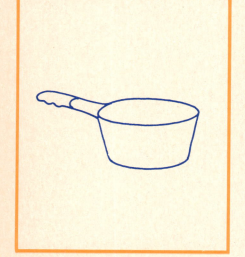

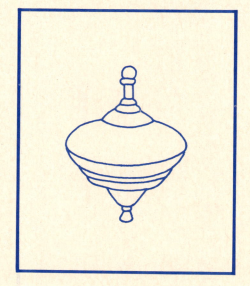

Initial M

4

Initial G, M, F, and R

5

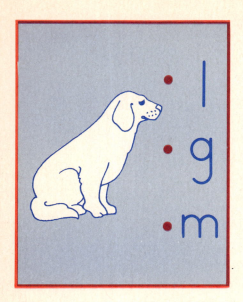
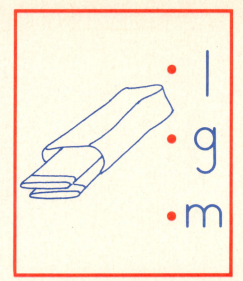

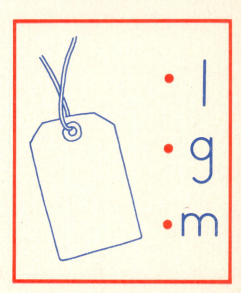
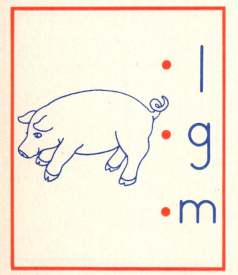

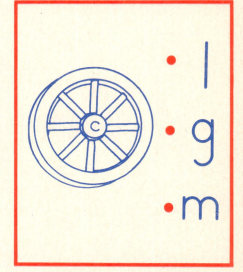

Final L, G, and M

6

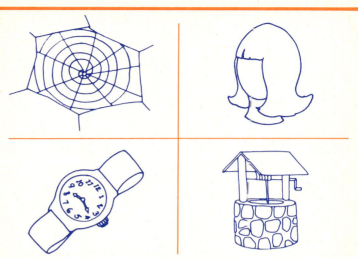
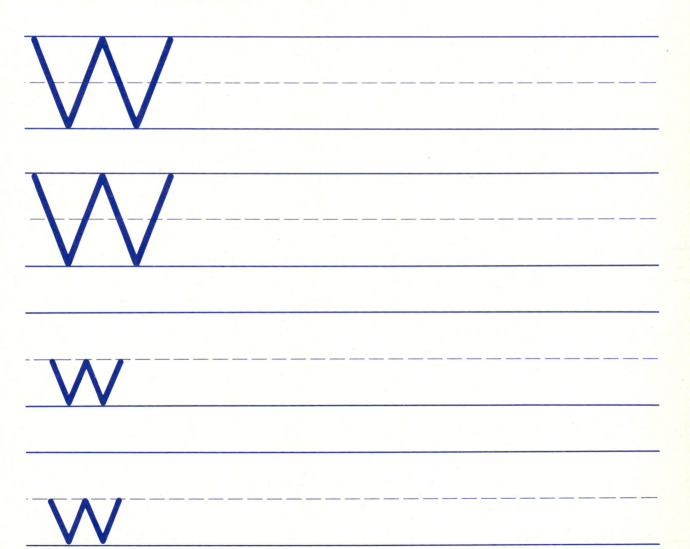

Initial W

7

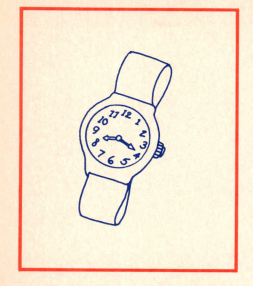  
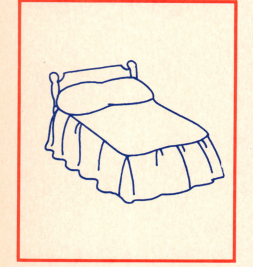 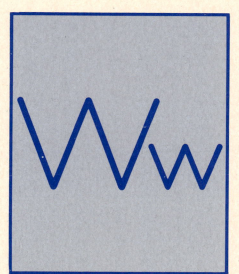 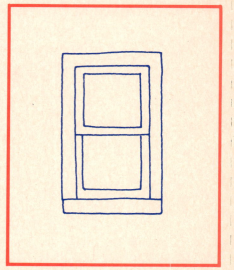
 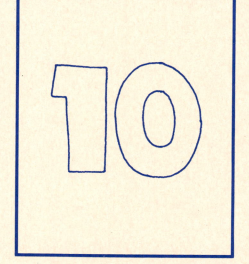 

Initial W

8

Mm

 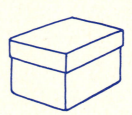 

Gg

Ww

  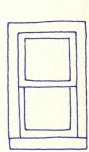

Initial M, G, and W

9

Initial J
10

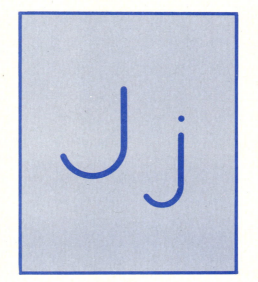
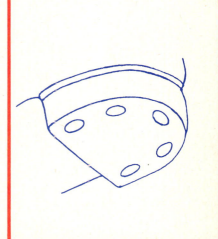

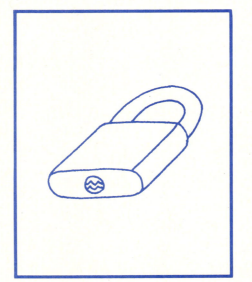

Initial J
11

Initial M, W, and J

12

G M W J	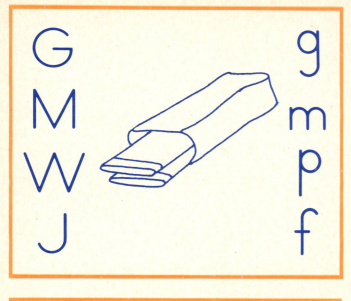	g m p f
G M W J		g m f t
G M W J		g m b d
G M W J		g m t n
G M W J		g m b p
G M W J		g m s r

Reviewing Initial and Final Sounds

13

W J F D L B C S

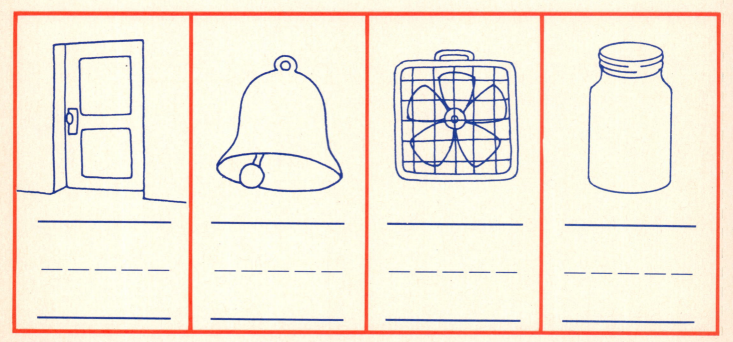

Reviewing Initial Sounds

14

s m g r d t l b f

Reviewing
Final Sounds

15

Reviewing Initial
and Final Sounds

16

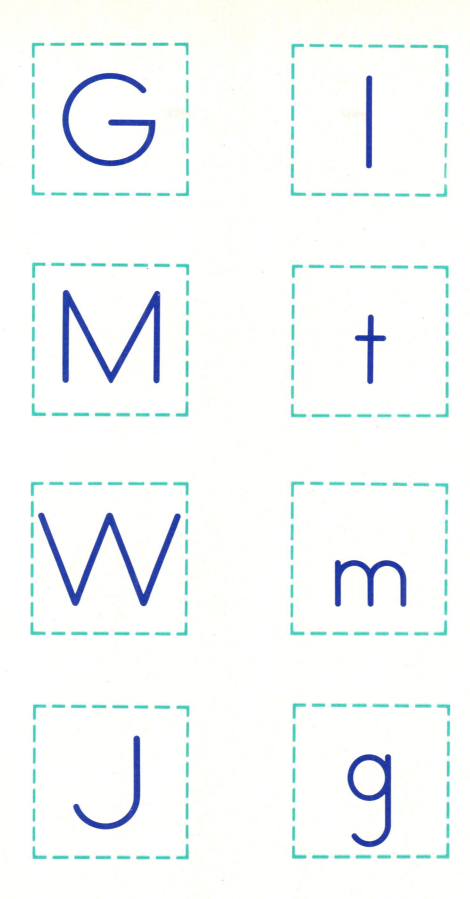

Reviewing Initial and Final Sounds

17

Initial K
19

Initial K
20

Reviewing
Initial J, W, and K

21

Initial V

22

Initial V
23

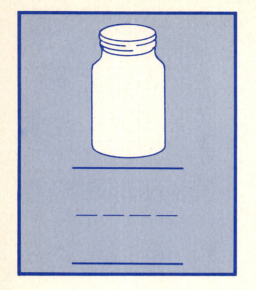
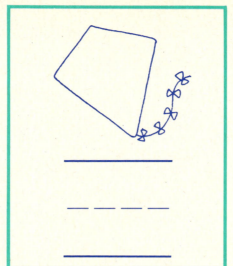
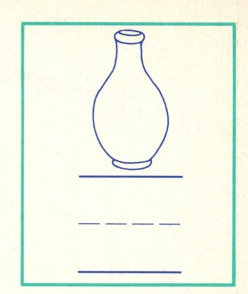
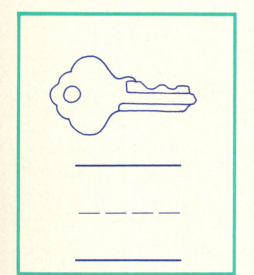
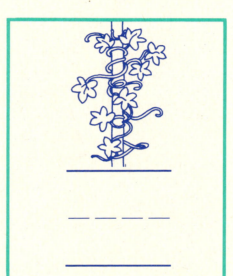

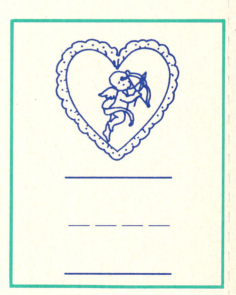

**Reviewing
Initial J, K, and V**

24

Reviewing
Final G, K, and V

25

Initial N
26

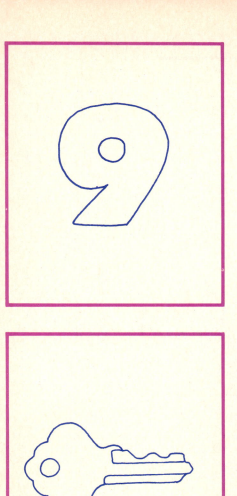

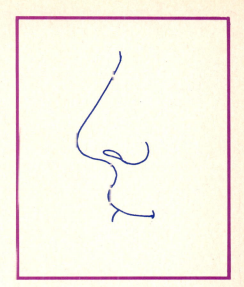
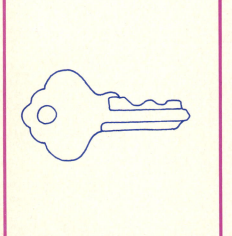
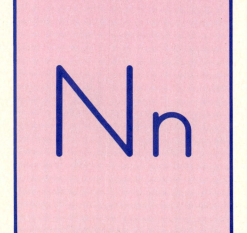
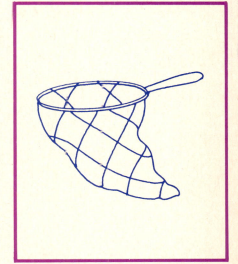
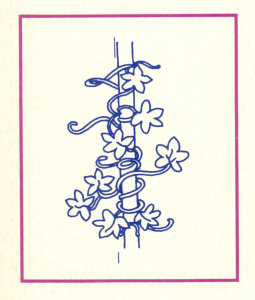

Initial N
27

Discriminating Initial M and N

28

**Discriminating
Final M and N
29**

Initial Q
30

Q q

N n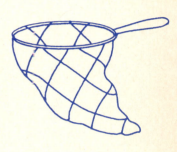

V v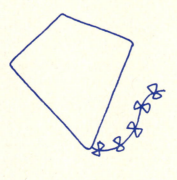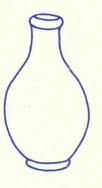

Initial
Q, N, and V
31

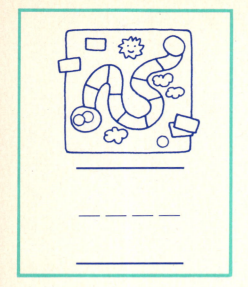

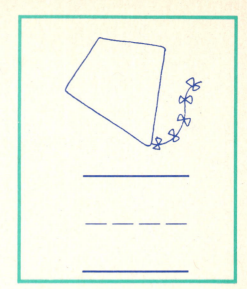

G M W
J K
V N Q

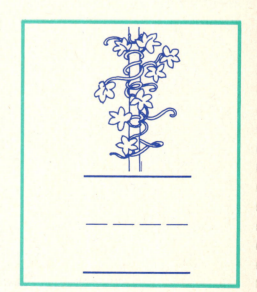

Reviewing Initial Sounds

32

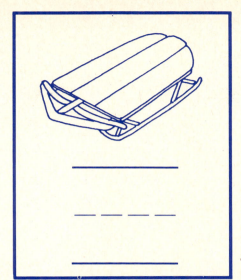

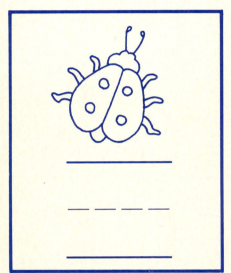

g m k
v n
f b d

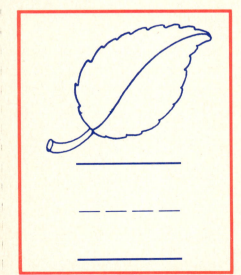

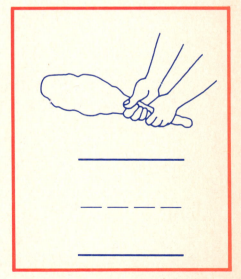

Reviewing
Final Sounds

33

Reviewing Initial and Final Sounds

34

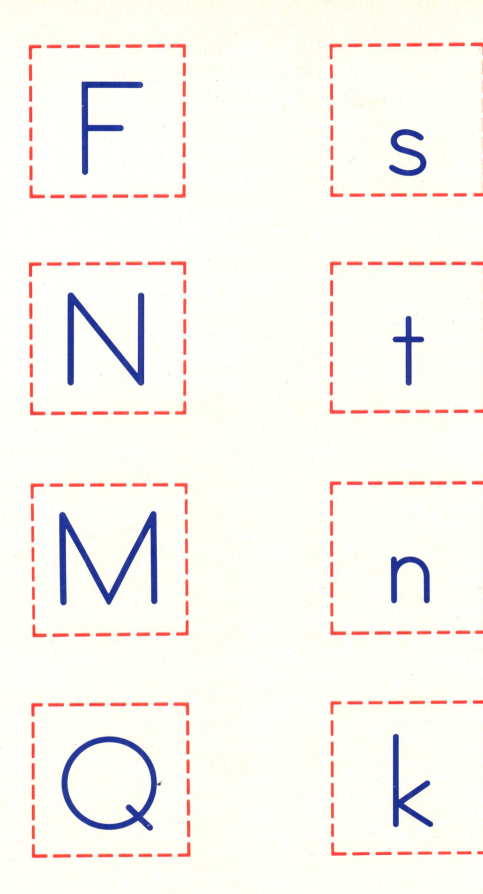

Reviewing Initial and Final Sounds

35

Y
Y
y
y

Initial Y
37

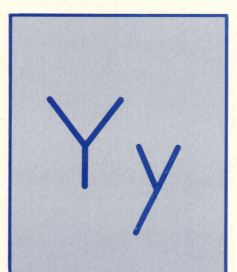
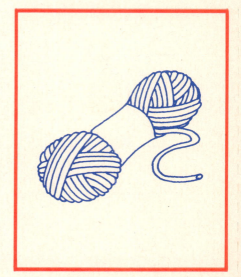

Initial Y
38

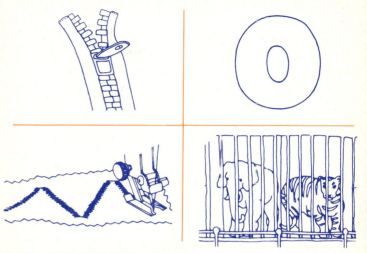

Z

Z

z

z

Initial Z
39

Initial Z
40

Initial Z, Y, and Q

41

Final X
42

Final X, G, and V

43

Reviewing Final Sounds

44

Reviewing Initial and Final Sounds

45

Reviewing Initial and Final Sounds

46

Reviewing Initial and Final Sounds

47